Internet Security

Online Protection From Computer Hacking

2nd Edition

By James Cloud

© **Copyright 2015 James Cloud - All rights reserved.**

In no way is it legal to reproduce, duplicate, or transmit any part of this document in either electronic means or in printed format. Recording of this publication is strictly prohibited and any storage of this document is not allowed unless with written permission from the publisher. All rights reserved.

The information provided herein is stated to be truthful and consistent, in that any liability, in terms of inattention or otherwise, by any usage or abuse of any policies, processes, or directions contained within is the solitary and utter responsibility of the recipient reader. Under no circumstances will any legal responsibility or blame be held against the publisher for any reparation, damages, or monetary loss due to the information herein, either directly or indirectly.

Respective authors own all copyrights not held by the publisher.

Legal Notice:

This eBook is copyright protected. This is only for personal use. You cannot amend, distribute, sell, use, quote or paraphrase any part or the content within this eBook without the consent of the author or copyright owner. Legal action will be pursued if this is breached.

Disclaimer Notice:

Please note the information contained within this document is for educational and entertainment purposes only. Every attempt has been made to provide accurate, up to date and reliable complete information. No warranties of any kind are expressed or implied. Readers acknowledge that the author is not engaging in the rendering of legal, financial, medical or professional advice.

By reading this document, the reader agrees that under no circumstances are we responsible for any losses, direct or indirect, which are incurred as a result of the use of information contained within this document, including, but not limited to, —errors, omissions, or inaccuracies.

CONTENTS

Introduction
Chapter 1 – Internet Security And History
    Malware and Viruses
    Spam and Phishing & Hacking
    Digital footprints
    Unsecure Wi-Fi Connection
Chapter 2: Unsecured Networks
    Why you shouldn't connect to networks that are unsecure?
    How to use Wi-Fi hotspot securely?
Chapter 3 –Cookies
    What do Cookies Do?
    When are Cookies Created?
    How Long Does a Cookie Last?
    Who Can Access Cookies?
    How secure are Cookies?
    Types of Cookies
        Session cookie
        Persistent cookie
    What are Malicious Cookies?
    Viewing & Removing Cookies
    First and Third-Party Cookies
    Benefits of Deleting Cookies in a Computer
        Faster Performance
        More Disk Space
        Enhanced Security
    Using Google Chrome
    Using Firefox
    Using Safari
    Internet Explorer
    Using Opera
Chapter 4: Digital Footprints
    Websites and Online Shopping

    Social media
    Laptops, Tablets and Mobile phones
    How big is my Footprint?
Chapter 5 – Use of Anti-virus Software
    Importance of using an antivirus
    Why should you update your Antivirus frequently?
        There are new threats emerging every day.
        Virus protection is crucial for protecting your documents
        A Hacker Could Have Turned Off Your Updates
        You Could Infect Your Friends
Chapter 6 – Using a VPN And Other Internet Tools
    Other Internet Tools
    Spybot
    Pop Up Blockers
    Setting your browser settings
Chapter 7 – Social Networking Sites
    Security threats on social media
Chapter 8 – Email accounts
    Phishing expeditions
        Everything you need to know about spam
    Spam and Viruses
        Effects of spam
        Tips to avoid spam
Chapter 9 - Downloads And Online Fun
    Protecting your data
Chapter 10: Keyloggers
        How would one get a keylogger?
        How can one detect a keylogger?
    Hardware:
    Software:
    Kernel/driver:
        Defending Against Keyloggers
    Anti-Keylogging Software Options

Chapter 11: Do's and Don'ts of Internet security
Conclusion

Introduction

The Internet is an extremely useful part of our everyday world. However, it is also becoming increasingly dangerous. In the past, the only way that you could find the amount of information that you needed would have been through reading, and although reading is still very much involved in knowledge learning, the Internet makes looking things up very much easier than it ever was. People make purchases online as well and the market is huge. With companies from all over the world, how can you be sure that you are safe? It's a huge opening up of a potential "can of worms" although if you know how, you can stay safe.

Internet speeds have also increase from 128 Kbps to an amazing 1 Gbps over the past twenty years and that's frightening with fiber offering speeds such that streaming TV programs has become something that people take for granted. What this also means though is that it's easier for you to be cheated if hackers get hold of your information.

Information passes at speeds, which are frightening. Life may seem like its giving people exactly what they need. However, safe Internet is not always viable, especially when left in the hands of inexperienced users who don't know enough to keep themselves safe. While switching on a computer may seem easy enough, what it does when it connects to the Internet is become part of a global village of networks which spread all over the world. In fact, every Internet user has an IP (Internet Protocol) or an address that connects to the server. This is the identity of your connection and sets you apart from other users.

There are an estimated 120 billion people in the world using the Internet and although you may consider yourself safe in the comfort of your home, don't be lulled into that kind of security. Hackers may be aware of what you are doing and use your data to get access to very personal information such as log-ins and bank account details. The trouble is that many users are helping them by not being vigilant enough.

It's important that each computer has built in security and that websites which are used for any payments should be secure websites so that users have a better idea of their security when using these sites. However, with as little information as your password, what's to stop a hacker accessing accounts where your credit card details are already registered? Sites such as Amazon have made it extremely easy for you to purchase things with just one click, but hackers who have your password can do the same thing.

You need to think of browser security and security of every bit of data that you use on the Internet. It may sound like it's fairly straightforward if you have a decent virus checker, but it's a little more complex than that.

An experienced Internet user who knows how to protect a computer against the threats that are posed today writes this guide. By following this guide, you will be able to adjust your computer, so that you can indeed enjoy your Internet use without worrying about who is hacking into your information or watching your activity.

Within its chapters, you should find sufficient information, written in an easy to understand manner, so that even those who have little experience will be able to follow the instructions and make sure that their computers are safe. That's important in a day and age when it is very likely that children will be using the computer at some time or other.

The last thing that you need to think about just before the holidays or at any time of year is whether your information is being used. Your credit cards and your logins should be safe but unless you take action, you cannot be confident that they are. People have even had identities stolen on the Internet, making it a very dangerous place indeed.

Chapter 1 – Internet Security And History

Whether you are an individual or have a company that uses the Internet, it's important that you protect your financial details at all times. Servers and network hardware secure the security of an Internet connection. If this is not secure, there is the possibility that companies could go bankrupt and that information which is confidential data could get into the wrong hands. Even the military connects to the Internet, so you can see that any breach of security would be more harmful than one could possibly imagine.

The first thoughts of Internet Security predate the Internet, when people actually thought of what could potentially happen if data sharing every came into being. McAfee came up with a solution as far back as 1987 though Virus Scan has of course been updated many times since the original programs were released

At this time, all computers sold in shops include virus protection as standard although what shops will not take responsibility for is those users who do not extend their virus protection once the free trial period has run out. The thing that confuses a lot of Internet users is what is the difference between paid and free anti-virus protection? Before you can answer that, you need to know what you need to be protected from.

Your Internet security depends upon several things and it's vital to take account of all of these. For example, while a virus may come onto your computer through malware, you may also leave yourself open to a clever virus by downloading files that have hidden content that you are not expecting. Let's go through some of the things that users need to protect themselves from and these include:

Malware and viruses

Spam and Phishing

Digital footprints

Insecure Wi-Fi connections

Hacking and key logging

These all sound a little frightening and you have every right to be frightened and should protect you from each of these elements. Before we explain how to do this, let's go through an explanation of what each of these involve.

Malware and Viruses

These are programs written with the intent to intrude on your privacy and destroy information or even get information. These get onto your computer by some obscure means in some cases. You may simply be browsing a website which automatically sends malware to your computer, or you may download something relatively innocent and find that malware is included in the package. That's why you need protection on your computer at all times, as this really does make you vulnerable to attack.

Spam and Phishing & Hacking

You have probably heard the word "spam" and will be familiar with it in your email box. It's uninvited email, but be very careful. Spam acts in a way that may put your accounts in danger. It may not be from whom you think it is from and that makes Internet users very vulnerable. For instance, PayPal emails, which arrive asking you to click on a link and confirm your details, may not actually be from PayPal. The information that you subsequently give may be on a site, which looks very much like PayPal, but indeed it may not be. These kinds of emails have been used for a lot of major companies as hackers get more and more ideas of where they can get user information.

Phishing is a little bit like it sounds; hackers go on a fishing trip for information. They may be checking to see if someone uses their email. They may also be telling you that you passwords have been changed and sending you to a page where you can fill in details to put this right. We have explained how to tell the difference and how to avoid leaving yourself open to this kind of fraud in our later chapters.

Digital footprints

Although all of these phrases may be phrases that you have heard, you may not realize the implication of them and what they actually do in the way of harm. If you can imagine someone looking over your shoulder and watching every password, every credit card detail or every email address that you use, as well as seeing which sites you use, then this is pretty much what digital footprint is and you may not even know that you are leaving these behind you.

Unsecure Wi-Fi Connection

With so many people using hot spots and Internet cafes all over the world, what are the chances that these places have secured connections? What about if someone sits at the computer you used five minutes ago to access your emails? What information could they get hold of which could be harmful to you? You need to be aware of what that insecurity means to you.

When using the Internet in a public area, make sure of what virus protection they offer as this is important and also whether VPN connections are available as these may help you to hide your digital footprint, provided that you sign off when you have finished. Ask in a cafe what protection is available for you. It only takes a moment to ask and that may save you having your accounts hacked by the next person who sits at that computer.

It's vital for all Internet users to know how to keep themselves safe on the Internet and future chapters should help you do just that. Your security matters and protecting your family and loved ones is equally important. Explain to children the importance of keeping themselves safe.

Chapter 2: Unsecured Networks

First, we will see what an unsecure network actually is. The network is usually un-secure if there are no login credentials needed for accessing it. On unsecure networks, you can access the Internet without any password and login. These unsecure networks can be found in many places like airports and other places where people can access the Internet easily.

In general, there are two types of Wi-Fi networks that users can access. They are ad-hoc and the traditional access point networks. In an ad-hoc network, the devices will directly connect with each other. This is different in a traditional access point network and the devices connect to a central router. In an ad-hoc network, there is no need for an additional hardware or a router. You can connect your phones or laptops together without an additional hardware. This will create an ad-hoc network.

The free Wi-Fi network that you see at the airport is an ad

hoc network, which could probably be a prank. Whenever you connect to this network, you're basically connecting to a computer. And when you connect to that computer, your computer will broadcast the free Wi-Fi network and other computers within the range can connect to your computer. This is a bad idea as other people can access all of your private data from your computer.

This is one of the reasons why you shouldn't connect your computer to unknown networks. This is a specific scenario and there are many more like this. Now, we will look at a few more scenarios like this.

Why you shouldn't connect to networks that are unsecure?

Say you are in a cafeteria, bored. And you decide to check your Facebook account for killing time. Your mobile or laptop will show all the available networks and you may find an open and unsecure network. Say that you are connected to that network and started surfing. It is a good way to pass time, coffee and free Wi-Fi. What you may not know is that there may be a hacker waiting to take advantage of the free Wi-Fi well within the range, waiting for doing a Man in the middle attack. You will at least surf till you complete your coffee and that is enough time for him to hack into your account, access your private data like emails, bank accounts etc.

How to use Wi-Fi hotspot securely?

As you can see, it is very easy for a hacker to eavesdrop on your Wi-Fi. By following the steps, you can get some degree of security when using public Wi-Fi.

- Always see that you are on an encrypted connection when you login into a website from a public Wi-Fi. For this, you should make sure that the URL address begins with an https instead of the normal http.
- You should also make sure that your connection is encrypted throughout your online session. Many websites will use an encrypted login and will return you to a normal session after the login, leaving your connection vulnerable to hack. Facebook is an example for such website which uses an encrypted login at the beginning and returns you to a normal connection which is not secure.
- Many sites in the market give their users the option of staying on and on an encrypted connection throughout your session. If you wish to stay on a secure line when using Facebook you should simply select secure browsing from the security settings of your account.
- Logging in using a web browser will ensure an encrypted connection when you are checking your mail. In case of email through outlook, you should always ensure that the encryption settings are turned on in your POP3 or IMAP and SMTP accounts.
- It is advised not to use the FTP or other services, which are not encrypted.
- Another way to keep your online activities encrypted is to use a virtual private network.

- You should always remember that all the private networks possess similar vulnerabilities. Anyone connected to the same can eavesdrop on such networks. You can encrypt your Wi-Fi traffic by enabling the WPA or WOA2 security. This will obscure the actual communications. But you should keep in mind that if they have the password, they could snoop on the data packets of that network. If these securities are not used, user-to-user eavesdropping is possible. Small businesses in particular do not use the 802.1X enterprise security; this is particularly important for them.
- Whenever you are dealing with important tasks like online banking, it is advised that you do them from your house.
- It is always wise to use a secure connection, even if it costs a few extra bucks rather than using an unsecure or public network.
- You can use VPN if you want maximum security for your online sessions.

Chapter 3 – Cookies

Cookies are nothing but small files that are stored on the user's computer. There is specifically designed to store small amounts of data specific to particular websites and clients. The client computer or the web server can access cookies. Cookies allow the web servers to deliver a page, which is tailored for a particular user. The term cookie is given to describe a particular type of message that a web server gives to the web browser. Identification of users and to customize the webpages for them is the main purpose of a cookie. Cookies also save your site login information.

What do Cookies Do?

Whenever you visit a website using cookies, you are asked to fill a form of personal information like your email address, your name and your interests. All this information will be packed into a cookie and this cookie will be sent to your web browser so that it can be used later when you visit the same website next time. At your second visit, the browser will send this cookie to the server. Every time the web browser requests for a page, the message will be sent to the server.

Cookies provide a convenient way of carrying information from different sessions on the website. These can also be used in between sessions on websites that are related. With the use of cookies, the servers are saved from the burden of huge amounts of data storage. It is also problematic to store the data on the web server without cookies, as it will be difficult to retrieve the information of a particular use, without the need of a login on each visit to the site. In cases where there is large amount of information to be stored, the cookie will be used for identifying a particular user so that more information can be looked up on the server side database.

For instance, when a user visits a site for the first time he may select a username, password, give his email ID, select the page layout and fonts size etc. and all of these will be stored inside a cookie. When the same user visit the site for the second time, the server will read the cookie from the user's computer and identifies that user. All the information about that user will be retrieved relieving the pain of re-entering the information.

A web server has no memory so the website that you are visiting will transfer a cookie of the web browser on your computer so that the site can identify you and a preferences that you have set. With this exchange of messages, web servers can display your customized web pages when you visit their website. For example, when you visit a website, instead of the regular welcome page you might get to see a different welcome page displaying your username.

When are Cookies Created?

Usually, whenever a new webpage is loaded, data will be written into a cookie. For instance, after pressing the submit button, the storing of values into the cookies is taken care by the data handling page. In cases, where the user disabled the cookies, the right operation will fail and the sites, which depend on cookies, will request the user to enter the information again or will take a default action.

How Long Does a Cookie Last?

When a cookie is created, the time of its expiry can also be set. The default expiry time for a cookie is when the current browser session ends. But it can be said to persist for a defined length of time.

Who Can Access Cookies?

By setting the root domain of a cookie, you can control its visibility. Any URL that belongs to that root can access that cookie.

For example, if the root is set to "whatarecookies.com", the sites "whatarecookies.com" or "xyz.whatarecookies.com" or "www.whatarecookies.com" can access this cookie.

This can be used to allow the related pages to exchange messages with each other. You're not allowed to set the domains for '.com' or '.co.uk' etc. as they are considered as 'top-level' domains and are using them will allow a widespread access to that cookie.

Though the cookies are visible by default to all the parts in their domains, they are restricted to a particular subpath during their time of creation. For example "www.whatarecookies.com/images".

How secure are Cookies?

The security and privacy of a cookie are of a major concern. Since cookies are only used for storing information, which was voluntarily added by the user, or given by the web server, they do not possess a threat to the user's privacy. In some cases these cookies can be accessed by some third-party websites and it is equally worse as storing them in a central database. If you're concerned about the information you provided would not be confidential, you should question yourself whether you really need to provide your information in the first place.

Types of Cookies

There are two types of cookies and they are.

Session cookie

A session cookie is also called a transient cookie. This cookie only exists tell the web browser is open. Once you close the web browser, this cookie will be erased. Session cookies are not stored in permanent memories but are stored in temporary memory. This cannot be retained once you close the browser. The session cookies will not collect the information from your computer. In a session cookie, the stored information will be in the form of session identification and it cannot identify the user.

Persistent cookie

A persistent cookie can also be called as a stored cookie or a permanent cookie. These cookies will be stored on the hard disk of your computer until they expire at their expiration date or until they are deleted. Unlike session cookies, the persistent cookies store any identifying information of the user. This information includes user preferences for specific websites, web surfing behavior etc.

What are Malicious Cookies?

Normally, cookies never compromise security but nowadays there are a lot of malicious cookies. Malicious cookies store your online activities. The cookies, which track the activities online, are defined as tracking cookies or malicious cookies. There are some commercial websites, which include advertisements that are served from third party sites and they can add cookies to the site, which contains the information of the containing site. The name of the site, the pages visited, products being viewed, etc might be included in such information. Having these cookies on your computer is not safe as they track your surfing habits over a given period of time and based on that they will build a profile with your interests. And once the tracking is complete, the gathered information can be sold to advertising companies who later use this information to target you with things that interest you. Many people find these tracking cookies as an invasion of their privacy because they help the advertiser by giving them the user profiles without their knowledge or consent.

There are many antivirus programs, which flag suspicious adware or spyware cookies when your system scanned for viruses.

Viewing & Removing Cookies

The web browser stores the cookies on the hard disk of your computer. If you wish to see the list of sites that are associated with your cookie files, you can view the cookies.

If you are using the Microsoft Internet explorer for browsing, you can have your cookies by selecting the Internet options from the tools menu. You can see a section with the name Browser History on the general tab. Click on the Settings and select the View Files option.

A Windows Explorer window will be displayed and the list of your temporary Internet files will be given. Those also include cookies. Every cookie will be given a different URL site with which they can be easily determined. You can decide the cookies which you want to keep and which you trust. If there are any cookies, which you don't recall from visiting the site, you can delete it.

First and Third-Party Cookies

The terms "first party cookies" and "third-party cookies" can be seen when you are choosing your privacy settings on your web browser. The first party cookies can be defined as the cookies which originate from the website which you are viewing currently. The first party cookies usually contain your preferences for that site. The third-party cookies originate from the website which is not your current site.

You can simply block all cookies but surfing the web without cookies will be difficult. For instance, if you are shopping online, most e-commerce shopping carts which are implemented with the cookies. When you disable or delete a cookie of a web site, your personalized references will not be shown when you visit that website. This means that you should start filling your information from scratch.

Despite off some misconceptions, most of the cookies are legitimate files. Cookies do not invade your privacy. Once you get used to the reviewing of cookies that are associated with your web browser and manage them by removing the delicious cookies or by trying different privacy settings on your browser, you can keep the normal cookies which make your surfing easy, yet keep the malicious cookies which track your surfing habits off your computer.

Benefits of Deleting Cookies in a Computer

Irrespective of the type of computer you are using, it is very important to properly maintain your system. A part of that maintenance is removing the unnecessary files like temporary Internet files and cookies. The benefits of removing the unnecessary files are many and some of them include better security, faster performance of your system, increase in the available space in your hard disk etc.

Faster Performance

Even though cookies are small files, they can build up and can result in slowing down of your system's performance. When there are too many cookies accumulated, all these unnecessary files can slow down your system's performance. By spending some time for deleting the temporary Internet files and unnecessary cookies, you can directly increase the performance and speed of your web browser.

More Disk Space

You should always ensure that there is sufficient space on your hard disk and deleting unwanted cookies regularly will free up your hard disk space. Your system's performance will automatically decrease if there is less space on your hard disk. In some situations the system may crash. The operating system will use the space in your hard disk to mimic the physical memory, and if the memory is insufficient, the system's performance will suffer. By deleting cookies you are increasing your hard disk space, which in turn increases your computer's performance.

Enhanced Security

Although most of the cookies are harmless, there are other cookies, which track your moves on the Internet. The tracking cookies are often used by businesses with the intent of studying the behavior of the consumer and many computer users think of it as an invasion of their privacy. You can set your web browser to clear cookies every time you exit your web browser and this will reduce the risk of security breaches.

It's a good idea to get into the habit of deleting your Internet history. If you get into this habit, what you are doing is making sure that those who use the computer after you will have no idea what sites you have been visiting. Remember to log out of all sites where you have been logged into personal information before you perform this task. There are several ways to do this depending upon which browser is being used. I have used examples of popular browsers below, so that you have all the information that you need.

Using Google Chrome

Look at the top of the page to where it says "Tools" and access the tools menu. This gives you access to "options" and what you need here is to look "Under the hood." You will find that there is a privacy section and you should select the "show cookies" option. A new window should show you all of your browsing history and pressing, "remove all" will clear up everything that you did on that computer.

Using Firefox

The process is pretty similar as you have a "tools" option located in the menu bar. Once again, you need to get into the Options area and access the Privacy tab. In Firefox, it's actually easier to achieve. Simply tick the box, which says that cookies should be accepted from sites. That way, the cookies will disappear. You may wonder about someone enabling the cookies after you have finished with the computer, but this will only enable them from then onward, so your information is safe.

Using Safari

Safari is easy to use and in the menu, you simply need to access preferences. When this window shows, press where it says Privacy. From here you can set your preference to block cookies. There's one complex suggestion that you get and that's whether you want to select parties and advertisers always or never. Simply press, "Remove all cookies" and the computer will do the rest for you. Then click on done and you will know that your computer is safe.

Internet Explorer

Many public computers will use Internet Explorer, and it's easy to get rid of your browsing history and cookies using this browser. Press on tools at the top and then click onto the tab labeled "Security." From here, you will be able to delete all temporary files including your browsing history, passwords etc. Tick the boxes that you want to delete and delete history. It will ask you if you are sure, and you should follow through and stick with the computer until you are satisfied that all files have been deleted. To double check open a fresh browser and press the Control key on the keyboard which is labeled Ctrl and then the letter H at the same time. This will show up the history and there should be nothing there.

Using Opera

You can set up your tools in Opera to delete all of your cookies and temporary files at the end of each browsing session, by clicking onto the tools section and using the preferences area of the browser tools.

Whether you are working at home or in a strange environment, it's worthwhile getting into the habit of getting rid of this information. If you are at home and want to bookmark some pages before they disappear, you can do this very easily. Make sure you have saved the sites that you want for future reference, but always make sure that you have logged out. For example, if Amazon is one of your favorites, the last thing you want to find is that your five year old managed to buy up the games department by clicking and getting all your credit card information which automatically comes up when logged in.

Chapter 4: Digital Footprints

Daily, without our knowledge, most of our Internet use contributes to a growing portrait of who we are online. This portrait is more public than we think. Whenever we need any information, we look at the Internet and it seems like the Internet is looking back at us. Whenever we use websites for getting information, social sharing, send messages and emails, we always leave something behind. All that we leave behind on the Internet are called Digital footprints.

Digital footprints bring benefits and costs. For instance, digital footprints offer convenience to the users by saving the login time or auto fill the personal details which saves a lot of time without having to re type all the details. Most of the users realize that they are consciously sharing the information on social media or uploading pictures, some degree of privacy is lost there. There are always footprints that are created by default, simply by shopping online, searching the web or by enabling the location services. And one cannot manage something that he cannot see. This portrait will help the companies to target their content at the specific consumers and markets; this will also help the employers to look into your background.

Digital footprints help the advertisers to track the movements of the user across different websites. Just remember that you leave a digital footprint behind whatever task you do online. So, it is wise to know the kind of footprints you are leaving behind when working online and their possible effects.

You can never make your footprint count to zero but by following a few steps you can reduce the count of your digital footprints. With this, it is not difficult to manage your digital identity.

Basically, the digital footprint of a person or a user can be defined as the stuff or traces that he leaves behind as he uses the Internet. Comments that were made on social media, calls on Skype, application use and email records are all part of your online history and other people can see them or track them from a database.

Leaving digital footprints happens in many ways. Here are some of them.

Websites and Online Shopping

The retailers and product review sites often leave cookies. These cookies can be used for tracking your site-to-site moments with which targeted advertisements will be displayed on your computer or products that you have recently looked at online.

Social media

Every one of those tweets and Facebook comments leave a digital footprint behind. You should keep an eye on the privacy settings that are set by default on your social media accounts. These websites release new settings and policies, which will result in the increase in the visibility of your data. Most of us do not read the new policy agreements and simply click OK at the end. Always ensure you read what you say OK to.

Laptops, Tablets and Mobile phones

Some of the websites make a list of the devices with which you visit the sites and save that information to secure your account. Though it is for your security, you should understand that this information is about your habits. It gives out prominent information like what device you use etc, so it becomes easier for a hacker to target your specific device.

How big is my Footprint?

If you want to know how big your digital footprint is, you can use any one of the several tools that are available in the market. These tools can be easily accessed and you can add them to your computer. They constantly monitor and control your digital footprint. Google is among the companies which is most commonly accused for collecting the user data and rightfully so. One of the ways for measuring how big your digital footprint is to see how much the advertising companies are allowed to track your browsing habits. You may recollect not giving permission for any of these advertising companies. But sadly, some sites allow the advertising companies to place tracking cookies on your laptop or mobile. Cookies can be defined as small chunks of data that the web servers create. The web browsers are used to deliver these cookies and they are stored on your PC. Cookies will allow the websites, which you visit frequently to keep a track on your preferences and online patterns. With this, a personalized experience for every user is offered.

For example, you can try searching for coffee tables and access sites that sell these products online. After this, you will notice that there will be small pop up advertisements of various coffee tables flashing on your computer screen. This is all a result of the tracking cookies on your computer.

Another method for obtaining a simple estimate on your digital footprint is by making use of the Digital Footprint Calculator, this is the service provided by the EMC Corporation. The software is available for both Windows and Mac operating systems. This software will measure the user input on the frequency of photos and video uploads, emails, web browsing, phone usage and where you live in the world. This calculator will give you an actual file size of your Internet presence after submitting the estimates. The software also provides an additional option where you can create a ticker widget with which you can share your result on the web page; this will expand your footprint a little more in this process.

Here are 10 steps, which will help you to erase your digital footprint.

1. Search yourself

Searching is the customary practice done by the employers when vetting the applicants. The information given by the search engines like Google can be seen by other people and not just by you. Your future bosses can also see it and if they find anything unprofessional, it can scupper your career. If you run a search on your name, there is a high possibility of finding all the sites in which you have created your account. Do not forget to search images. The first step of taking control on your digital footprint is by getting an understanding on it.

2. Deactivate your old social media accounts and check for the privacy settings.

Facebook, Google+, LinkedIn, Twitter, MySpace, etc. are some of the social media sites which can be mined for taking personal information of the employees. If your privacy settings are not tight, the viewers can get a look at your pictures, status updates and posts. You should always remember that the web often forgets about the context and your tweets can be misconstrued. There is a possibility of events happened years ago hampering your current prospects. Although your personal life is separate from your professional life, your profile may cause interest in the people who are trying to know who you are now. You should always check the privacy settings of the accounts in which you are active. For example, if it is your Facebook account, you can go to the account settings present on the top right corner of your page and select the privacy option from the list. Here you can decide who can access your information and who can search you using your mobile number or email address etc.

In case of Twitter, by clicking on the top right corner of your profile you can get the settings. The settings provide you with a range of account options and you can also make your profile a private one. Not adding your last name or by using a different last name, you can completely hide your account.

3. Hide others, or add false information

When dealing with social media accounts, which hold the information that you prefer to keep quiet, honesty is not always the best policy. There are a few social media sites that do not allow the account holders to delete their accounts. Such sites only give an option to deactivate. In such cases, consider changing your email address, name and upload a general profile picture such as landscape before deactivating your account. Here, your main motto should be to change as much information as possible about you.

If they run a search on you, they can only see the latest information that you have added and your accounts will not be displayed. The sooner you delete or deactivate your old accounts, the better.

4. Contact webmasters

If there is public information about you posted by the websites, the best option to remove this information and is by contacting the Webmasters. You can send them a mail or call them and explain why you wish your information removed. You will have to confirm that you are the account holder by sending them a mail from a registered email address or by calling them from a registered mobile number. They will take care of the rest.

5. Unsubscribe from mailing lists

Mailing lists will lead a digital trail back to you. You can break these connections by unsubscribing. This will de-clutter your inbox as well.

6. Have a secondary email account

Some online services will require your email address to register before use. It is advised to create a secondary email account for registering for sites that insist upon sending you emails for marketing and sales pitches. With this you can ensure that your digital footprint is clean.

7. Consider the 'right to be forgotten'

In Europe, the 'right to be forgotten' was recently involved and it means that the search engines can be made to delete the links for the publicly available news items from the results. The IT giant Google has appealed for the ruling and many of the links were removed. This resulted in the creation of list the de-index pages.

8. Check e-commerce and retail accounts

If you are not using any of the retail accounts are like Amazon, eBay etc. consider removing your accounts and the financial data in them. Nowadays, we often hear about the cyber-attacks on the major retailers and services. There is no need for keeping the sensitive data saved on the company servers of the retailers if you're not using them anymore.

9. Cover your tracks

IT giants like Google and Apple recently revealed that they would enhance the basic encryption in the services they provide. With this, there is an increase in the number of simple ways to become less traceable.

You should always keep in mind that despite some business jumping and start-up claims on the anti-NSA bandwagon, there is no solution available that will be completely surveillance proof. However, for an average user, the incognito mode of Google Chrome, the private browsing in Internet Explorer and the private window in the Firefox browser are capable of limiting the tractable data such as cookies.

10. A fresh start

Though this is an extreme action, if needed, deleting all of your aforementioned services and deleting your inbox of your email are the best ways with which you can remove your digital footprint. Only a little will be forgotten but by falsifying your names in your social media accounts, setting your security settings tight, clearing your inbox in your email and your e-commerce accounts will contribute in wiping your presence from the web.

Chapter 5 – Use of Anti-virus Software

As you can probably guess, the best is total security, but you may not need it. If your Internet supplier offers protection as part of your package, you may only need the Premium anti-virus software to supplement the anti-virus software that your Internet supplier gives you. Total security is what usually comes with a computer when you buy it, and you will be reminded to update when the free trial has run out.

The following are recommended although your supplier may provide you with a different package. These are the most well known ones:

McAfee
Norton
K7
Bit Defender
Kaspersky

Each has their own quirks. For example, if you are a gamer, you may find that Norton will actively slow your computer down which is irritating when you are trying to kill aliens while McAfee seems to run better for gamers. There are free software packages available that also allow you to go into stealth mode, but be aware that these may need to be complemented by other programs to make up for any shortfall.

Avast
AVG

Both are well known and do update their information frequently, though the more comprehensive packages are more likely to catch those bad files being downloaded onto your computer. However, if you use a less comprehensive virus checker, there are several programs that can help you. One is K9 and it is a rather amusing program. If you try to download something and it thinks that there is something harmful in it, it will prompt you with a dog bark so you get the choice of whether you continue or not. It's a great program if you are prone to downloading software as much of the free software comes with hidden malware. This program helps you to keep your computer safe. There are various levels of protection that you can choose and that makes it a super easy program to use.

Another program to help clean up malware is CCleaner. It's a very good tool to have because it does all the work for you. Simply ask it to clean your computer of things that it believes to be superfluous and it does a marvelous job at keeping things clean. It's also got a very neat area for startup. If you are experiencing an annoyingly slow boot up when you turn the computer on, you can disable some of the programs, which load at start up and get your computer going faster.

Importance of using an antivirus

Every Internet and computer users, regardless of the reason for being online, should have the latest antivirus on their computers. Though most of the programs are provided by the operating system, an antivirus should be installed on your computer if you wish for uninterrupted and safe Internet usage. The antivirus software plays a crucial role in the safety of computers. You can save your files and vital documents from being lost forever or becoming damaged by using an antivirus.

Now we will look at how an antivirus software program effects and eliminates the potential threats on your computer.

All this can be done in one of two ways. There will be a virus dictionary where the definitions for all new and existing viruses are stored. The antivirus program on your laptop or PC will scan for viruses that match the definitions in the virus dictionary. If the antivirus software program files a match, it will notify the user about the threat and also suggests the action to be taken. Some antivirus software handles these threats even without notifying the user about them. The second method with which viruses are located involves the identification of suspicious virus behaviors like data capturing, spyware or Port monitoring. Whenever any of these behaviors is observed, the antivirus will come into play and takes care of the infected files. We often see that there are potential viruses and other spyware that spread through emails. Not all of these viruses are invisible. The attackers use advertising meant for spreading their viruses. When browsing, you may see a dialog box saying, "You have won $6 billion click here to claim" or something similar to that. Once the user clicks on that link, it will download a virus automatically onto your system. These viruses will then start attacking your system files and end up eliminating or damaging them. These threats can be minimized with the help of antivirus software. Installing an antivirus on your computer is just like locking the doors of your house or hiding valuable things in your safe. Similarly, the safety of your computer will depend on the efficiency of the antivirus software installed.

There are a few antiviruses that are freely available in the market which you can download free of cost and install them on your laptop or PC. Before downloading an antivirus, have a look at its reviews from other users. That will help you to know the advantages and disadvantages of that antivirus. Antivirus software like McAfee, BitDefender, Norton etc. are a few of the respected antiviruses in the computer security industry. These companies will frequently monitor for new viruses and will update their antivirus to face these new viruses. You should know that no antivirus software will assure the complete safety of your computer but they can reduce the risk of the viruses cause to a great extent.

Why should you update your Antivirus frequently?

Let us say that you have installed antivirus software and it scans for viruses. Let us also assure me that you have not updated your antivirus. So, can we now say that your computer is completely safe from all the viruses? The answer will be no. This is because there might be a few more viruses that are created after your anti-virus program is programmed. This means that the virus dictionary only holds the information on viruses that are discovered during its time and your antivirus will not have information on the latest viruses and it might probably consider it as normal file and not as a virus. By updating your antivirus, you are basically updating your virus dictionary. Updating your dictionary will help your antivirus find the latest threats. So, by constantly updating your antivirus, you can keep your system safe.

After installing and antivirus you need not update your antivirus manually. Almost all of the antivirus software comes with an auto update feature, which the user can turn on or off. It is advice to keep that on, as it will constantly look for updates and updates your antivirus whenever there is a new update released. Some of the reasons for updating and antivirus are given below.

There are new threats emerging every day.

Hackers and cyber criminals always look for new vulnerabilities and holes in the security of computers so that they can exploit to create much more powerful and new viruses. If your antivirus is not up-to-date, it only means that you are leaving yourself wide open for the attack, as it won't have the data regarding the latest viruses. Always remember that whenever a new virus is released, your antivirus becomes outdated.

Virus protection is crucial for protecting your documents

There are a few viruses and spyware on the Internet, which can hack into your computer and can easily correct or even delete your data. There are viruses that lock your information with a password that you don't know. If you store vital or sensitive information on your laptop or PC, having an antivirus protection is a must.

A Hacker Could Have Turned Off Your Updates

Let us say you have a door which will trigger an alarm when open the forcefully. Now there is a thief who disconnects the alarm and opens the door accessing all your belongings. The same thing can happen with computers. It is possible for someone to access your laptop or mobile and turn off the real-time monitoring feature, which downloads the updates automatically. This can be a case where the hacker is trying to compromise your security and it can be by accident sometimes. If you have set your antivirus to update automatically and feature has been turned off without your knowledge, you will still remain under the impression that your antivirus automatically downloads updates but in reality it doesn't. For this, you should always make sure that your antivirus has the latest update installed.

You Could Infect Your Friends

If your computer is infected with the virus, it affects not only your data but it can spread itself with the help of USB flash drives, network links or by email. This means that your computer can spread the virus to the network it is connected with or to any person whom you send an email to. You may end up inviting your friends or colleagues computers and this is all because you did not update your antivirus.

These are some of the reasons why you should update your antivirus constantly. Not updating your antivirus will leave your and your friends computers vulnerable to infection.

Virus protection is something that will protect your computer from viruses as long as it is present. It isn't something that you perform once and forget. Protecting your personal files on your computer from viruses is an ongoing activity. For non-stop protection, it is advised to frequently update your antivirus. This will ensure the virus protection against spywares, malware, viruses and other computer invaders.

Chapter 6 – Using a VPN And Other Internet Tools

For those who do not know what a VPN is, it's a very good firewall kind of program that gives you a different address from your real one. That means that even if someone is able to locate your IP address, they don't know where you are. They can only guess. Whether you are aware of it or not, some websites check to see which country you are in because they target their site toward certain geographical areas. Thus, if you have a VPN connection and choose an appropriate area, the Internet becomes more accessible to you.

A VPN is a private network, and companies will often use these backed up by their own servers. That means that the company business is private and cannot be snooped upon. From a business perspective that's very important as if customer information was to leak, this could pose a security threat to that company.

For the individual, it's a safe environment in which to work, provided that you take the same precautions as you would with any other website connection, having virus protection in place. Once you turn off the VPN, you go back to your normal IP address, but others who do not have permissions cannot get onto the VPN and that's great from a security point of view.

Using a VPN for banking and for other secure purchases online is helpful because it stops people being able to follow your traces. VPN has been used for a variety of purposes, not all of them honest, but it does give you access to programs that you would normally use in your country when you are away from home and that's a great benefit.

Other Internet Tools

AdAware is a good program that you can download from the Internet, which makes you aware when you have programs that have been loaded onto your computer without you actually realizing it. This means that you can eliminate them.

Spybot

Some of the most harmful program additions are spy programs attached to things that you download. These will get onto your computer, regardless of your anti virus software and Spybot, run once a week, will get rid of them. This is a great program to use and you don't have to have a lot of technical knowledge to use it. If you are always downloading programs or visiting odd websites, then this is a great addition to have on your computer.

Pop Up Blockers

Although many browsers have additional tools such as pop up blockers, some don't. If you find that you are plagued by pop ups, then investing in one of these is a good idea. If you use CT.net to search for a pop up blocker, many are free and run quietly in the background stopping you from being invaded by unwanted pop-ups. One thing to remember is that when you are on sites where you need the pop up, you need to press the control key on your keyboard, which will dis-activate it temporarily.

Setting your browser settings

If you have children using the Internet, you can set up your browser to high security so that the children cannot access items that are unsuitable. Windows has a great web page with full instructions <u>here</u> to help you keep your family safe while on the Internet.

Parents should be aware that children will be curious and will explore things that they think they can get away with. There is a section on child safety in a future chapter, because on social networking sites, they really need to know what's acceptable and what information may put them in danger.

Children are particularly trusting and that makes them very vulnerable indeed.

Chapter 7 – Social Networking Sites

There was a posting on Facebook last week that really made readers think. It went viral because of the importance of the message it sent.

Yet, people add strangers to their networks every single day. Why? It goes back to the old school-day thing of wanting to appear popular and having lots of "friends." The problem is that these people are strangers. Yet everyday people post things that allow others to know about their activities and movements. Look at these and there is an obvious flaw in the logic.

"I am in hospital all week and had no one to look after the dogs. Had to put them in a doggie hotel."

This tells potential thieves that the house is empty. It is just the kind of message that they want to see, especially if you filled out your profile in such a way that they could figure out exactly where you live. Even with the village name, it wouldn't take them long to find out which house is yours. It's a very worrying thing that people who you believe that you have come to trust may be just the people who will cheat you or will do you harm.

On social networking sites, it's important to give out as little personal information as you can. For example, do you really want strangers to know which restaurant you are in at what time? Do you want them to know that you are out at work? As far as children are concerned, they should be told that they should only befriend those people that they know offline because there are some pretty bad people out there pretending to be something that they are not, in order to attract young people. A pep talk on things such as this would be in order when children start to use the Internet.

While a child may just want all of his friends to see his pictures, he must be shown how to make his group of friends private so that others cannot see those pictures. Did you know that a child on a skateboard might be a perfect invitation to a pedophile? It may have buildings in the background that are recognizable. It may show the time of day. What that tells the pedophile is that you are playing in that vicinity at a set time, making you a target.

From a work point of view

If you think that your Facebook, LinkedIn and other social networking site comments are private, think again. Unless you set your account up correctly, a future employer could find that your activity on these websites shows that you are unsuitable as a potential hire. That means that the fun you have on the Internet isn't as funny any more.

Be careful when you interact with others. Even pen pal sites have been known venues for people to be ripped off. The beautiful blonde who wants to marry you is so perfect that you think yourself a very lucky guy. Wait until she asks you for the fare to come to America to see you. It's unlikely that she will ever arrive, even though the two of you seem to be hitting it off. Believe it, people out there are out to take you for everything you have. Don't allow this kind of thing to happen.

Security threats on social media

Our interaction with friends and acquaintances has changed dramatically through social networking. Social networking sites like Facebook, YouTube, and Twitter etc.; play a huge role in connecting people, but also pose security threats to their users.

These social networking sites have millions of users, who use them regularly, to be in touch with friends and family. Alongside, there are also people who lurk around online trying to gather information about you and your online activity; often with a malicious intent. Hence, it is important that you stay safe from such security threats. Here are the five online threats that you should be wary of.

1. Theft of your identity

The main intent of identity thieves is to collect your personal information by stalking you on social networking sites. Even with the robust security settings of your account, it is possible for the identity thief to gather information about you using various strategies. Most of the prominent social networking websites require you to submit your email id, contact number, date of birth etc; for creating an account.

If the identity thief gets hold of your email address, he can hack it using various password-cracking tools. Then, he tries to hack your social networking account by clicking on the 'forgot password' button and when the login information is sent to the email, he gets holds of it, logs in and takes control of the social networking account. Thus, if a thief succeeds in hacking your email account, he will easily gain access to all the social networking sites connected to the email.

Once he gains access to your social networking account, he steals or modifies your personal information that is private only to you and your friends.

So, how can you stay safe from such online threats? It is not necessary for you to panic and delete or deactivate your social accounts; all you need to do is follow the precautions given below:

- Do not use weak passwords for your social accounts. Stronger passwords are harder to guess. Don't just use lowercase letters to create a password; your password should be a combination of numbers, lowercase letters, uppercase letters and symbols. Also, refrain from using your personal information as your passwords i.e. your name, birthday, your kid's name, spouse's name, name of your workplace etc, as they are easy to guess once the attacker gets hold of your personal information.

- See that your status updates do not reveal personal information to the public. Posting a casual status innocently is enough for an identity thief to get hold of the information he wants for stealing your identity. For example, you may just make a post wishing your mother on her birthday and tag her in the post. The "Happy birthday dear mom" post may look so innocent and adorable but it gives out more information than you think. When you tag your mother in the post, most likely, it is possible to get hold of her maiden name. A commonly asked security question while trying to login to an account is "what is your mother's maiden name?" and if the identity thief could answer the question, he can gain entry into your account. Also, the post reveals your mom's birthday, which raises the risk of your mom's account getting hacked.

- See that your location is not revealed in your posts or profile. It is safe to specify a fake location or it could even be just left blank. See that you do not mention where you live.

2. Your computer getting infected through malicious links

Shortened links are common on social networking sites like Twitter, where the number of characters allowed in a post is limited. Hackers make use of shortened URLs and mislead users into visiting malicious websites, through which viruses can be injected into your system. Sites like bit.ly are used to create shortened URLs, which are vulnerable to hackers. As the users cannot see the full URL, they can be tricked into visiting spoofed sites where they are duped to give away personal/confidential information.

The best thing to do is to refrain from clicking on a link unless you are positive that the link leads you to a trusted source. You can follow the steps given below to know if a link is safe or not:

- A simple rule to follow before clicking on a link is to hover over it with the cursor. When you hover over the link, the actual URL is displayed at the bottom corner of the web browser. If you identify the website and are sure that it can be trusted, proceed and click on the click.

- There are websites called link scanners, which check whether a URL is safe, or not. All you have to do is enter the URL you are suspicious of, and the website tells if it is safe or not. Examples of such link scanners are URLvoid, MyWOT etc.;

- As mentioned earlier, websites, which help in creating, shortened URLs, such as TinyURL, bit.ly and Ow.ly. Services like Sucuri can be used check if the actual link is safe or not.

You might ask, *"My PC doesn't contain anything important, why would anyone hack it?"*

While it may be true that your personal computer contains not more than a handful of illegally downloaded music or movies, it doesn't necessarily mean your PC won't interest hackers. Even if your computer does not contain any important, confidential or sensitive information, a hacker might attack it and bring it under his control. Once your PC is hacked, its IP address can be used to commit cybercrimes or to perform illegal online activities.

3. Unintentionally revealing information to stalkers

Cyber stalking (online stalking) is a major problem on social networking sites. Even though the settings allow you to block a stalker from viewing your profile, the stalker can simply create a fake account to stalk you again. So, you should be careful not to reveal personal information through your posts. Once you post something personal online for the public to see, you are inadvertently handing out your personal information to stalkers. Even under tight privacy settings, information leak is inevitable. For example, even the pages you 'like' or the products you 'like' will reveal information about you. Social networking sites offer online games and apps, which when used, collects information about you.

4. Sharing your whereabouts online for the burglars to notice

It is great that you are on a vacation with your family or having fun on a night out with your friends or heading to a slumber party with your buddies, but sharing such news online is anything but smart. Announcing your travel plans or your whereabouts online is nothing less than sending free invitations to burglars to break into your house. An average burglar will need only a few minutes to break into your house and a few more minutes to invade your privacy and steal your belongings. By announcing online that you are having a great time with your spouse in the Bahamas, you are unintentionally giving away information like your absence at your home, the length of your trip etc; to potential burglars. Burglars love it when you constantly update your whereabouts, so that they can sketch their housebreaking plans conveniently. Would you stand in public and yell at the top of your voice about your vacation plans? Of course you wouldn't. But, that is what you are doing when you merrily announce your travel plans online.

Here are a few things to remember when you take a vacation:
- Do not post your holiday pictures online while you are still holidaying. It is advised that you contain your

excitement and wait till you get home to share them online.

- If you must post your pictures while still holidaying, use the highest possible privacy settings for sharing them. See that only your close friends and family can view them.

- Don't go into the details; you don't have to let the whole world know that you are going to catch the plane on a particular day, or that you are going to return home on a particular day.

- It is ok for you to feel homesick and miss your friends, while you are on a business trip away from home. But it is not ok to share the same publicly on your wall. Burglars are smart enough to deduce that you are away from home, by looking at your emotional 'I miss home' posts.

- Stay away from social networking while holidaying. After all, it is a vacation. It's a great chance for you to just relax and contemplate the scenery around you.

One should be extra cautious while posting on social networking sites. Your social account should never be like an open diary, it should be just a means for you to be in contact with your dear ones. It is advised that you do not reveal the following information in your posts or profiles:

- Bank account information (For instance, taking a picture of your debit card or credit card and posting it online. Yes, there are actually people who do that.)

- Your house address (Unless you want to catch the attention of socially active and enthusiastic burglars or trespassers)

- Travel/vacation plans (Again, unless you want to notify potential housebreakers of your absence)

- Information about your children (like their names, school name, date of birth etc. ;)

- The name of your work place and its location (unless it is a professional network site like LinkedIn and you are positive you don't have any serious stalkers who would show up near your workplace the next morning)

- Your daily routine/schedule (You hit the gym every Wednesday and Friday at 7AM? Great, but that should go into your personal calendar, not onto your Facebook wall.)

Social networking sites sure are fun and entertaining, and sometimes even useful, but it is necessary that you be cautious of how safely you are going to use them.

Chapter 8 – Email accounts

There are so many different kinds of email account these days, but each kind has its vulnerabilities. For example, if someone gains access to your email account, they may also be able to gain access to the following:

> PayPal Account
> eBay account
> Your account at Amazon
> Your account on any online store

It's very unlikely that a thief could gain access to bank details since banks are not in the habit of sending personal information by email. You may be asking how they would have access. With access to your email account, all they have to do is access the sites mentioned and press forgot password. They open up the reminder from the site allowing them to reset the password. Once this is done, you may be totally unaware of it, but someone could be buying a lot of things using your account. The safeguard that you have is that you may be able to get access to information, which indicates where the goods went, but most thieves are clever and will have wiped out the address from your address book by the time you find that the money has been taken out of your account.

Phishing expeditions

Mass emails may be sent out to thousands of potential email addresses. Never respond to one because you are in effect telling the sender that, yes, that email account is used currently. Another rule that's very important especially when getting emails from PayPal, eBay or other companies that you have dealings with is never to click the links in the email. These links may take you to websites not even associated with PayPal or eBay but which look very similar. If you have a doubt, access PayPal or eBay direct from your search page, log in and see what emails you have in your message box. If you don't have any, delete the email you received and thank your lucky stars you have the good sense to do so.

Clicking on links in phishing emails is really bad form. They may lead to all kinds of circumstances. This is the way that viruses can be spread. If you do not know the sender, do not click the links. Even if you do know the sender, do not click them if they make no sense to your conversations.

There are websites, which give full information about scams, and it's always a good idea to read up on these. The latest Phishing tactics are to telephone you at home and tell you that you have a serious virus on your computer. The people who telephone purport to be from Microsoft and although you may think yourself important enough for Microsoft to care about, think sensibly. These people want you to give them access to your computer and will talk you through the process. If you do get calls such as this, simply put down the phone.

Your information

When you set up your email account, you probably didn't think that you would be corresponding with strangers. Most people don't. They open an email to correspond with family and friends. Although you have a space in which to put a signature and it's nice to sign off your emails in a nice way, remember not to include your address or your telephone number in this signature. You wouldn't give it to strangers.

The offer that's too good to be true

> Want to slim without even trying?
> Want to get a free iPhone?
> Want to earn a fortune online?

Step lightly. Reading the small print is worth more than simply taking free samples for granted as being "free" as sometimes they are not as free as they appear to be. The email senders are depending upon your vanity and your vulnerability.

Everything you need to know about spam

A spam email can be defined as a form of economically viable commercial advertising as it is a highly cost-effective medium for the advertiser. Spammers gain the addresses of the recipients from publicly absolute sources. They make use of the programs for collecting the addresses on the web and use dictionaries for making automated guesses by adding to user names that are common in a given domain.

In many countries, spamming is politically debated and in some places spamming is legislated with varying results. For circumventing the laws, anti-spam lists that are used by the anti-spam software and service provider regulations; spammers often forge or conceal the origin of the messages they send.

About 95% of the emails sent worldwide are believed to be spam mails. This makes the tools for spam fighting increasingly important for the users.

Spam and Viruses

The computers, which are infected by virus, are most likely to send spam messages. Spammers and virus makers are putting their efforts together for compromising the innocent computer users systems and they are converting those systems into spam sending "zombies" or "drones". These malicious programs spread rapidly and they can generate a huge number of spam mails, which look like they are sent from legitimate addresses.

It is recommended for all users to install and maintain an antivirus so that they can avoid their computers from being infected and become a source of spam without their consent.

Effects of spam

Apart from the junk mails that are being sent to the inboxes of millions of random and innocent users, these spam mails can have a serious effect indirectly on the email services and its users.

A wide number of email users are affected by default-defined messages that claim to be coming from the service's administrators. Most of these mails contain messages stating that their accounts are locked and they require some kind of action by the account holder to reopen their accounts. Most of these messages contain viruses and these mails should be deleted or ignored.

Tips to avoid spam

Education is considered to be an integral part of the security. By educating yourself or your employees, you can effectively defend yourself against such attacks and in some cases you can also save money. Some part of your bandwidth costs are consumed by these spam messages and by educating yourself you can protect your email address which results in lesser spam mails. You may not find a difference if you are the only user but in cases where there are a number of people who use the same connection, the difference can be seen clearly. This will in turn help you to reduce your bandwidth costs and save some bucks.

Here are some tips with which you can protect yourself from spam messages. If you are a part of an organization, conveying these steps to all the members of your organization could possibly help you reduce the amount of spam mails received.

1. When you are posting on forums, it is advised not to include your email address as a part of your signature.
2. Guest books are a major source for spammers and harvesting the email addresses. Some of the guest books will automatically hyperlink your email address to your username. Your work email should never be used for these kinds of personal uses. If there is no alternate email address, you can always use the free services such as Yahoo mail, Hotmail or Gmail. In cases where you must add your email address, you can use a disposable one or you can obfuscate your address by using instance words in place of the special characters ("AT", "DOT", etc.).
3. You should never use your work email when signing up for offers, forums and other public services. You can also use a disposable email address if it is well within the terms of rules. If the rules don't permit the use of disposable email address, you can always go for the free email services, which have spam filtering.

4. You should always be careful not to click on the links that you see in a spam email. In some cases where you click on the links, a confirmation message will be sent to the spammer saying that it is a valid email address. This will make the user a prime target and more of those spam messages will be sent to him.
5. It is wise to review the terms of privacy on the websites before registering. You should always ensure that whomever you are a signing up with would keep your information confidential. If third parties get hold of your email address, they might even sell your email address.
6. Always be careful not to display your email address publicly in cases where you use chat rooms and IRC.
7. Spammers use scanners for harvesting such emails. Using the free email services is the best for these purposes.
8. You should not to click on the unsubscribe link displayed in the spam mails. This is also method of confirmation that spammers use for confirming if your email address is a valid one.
9. You should not open or download the attachments from spam, as they may infect your computer with Trojans. Trojans will send your contacts to the spammer and trap you in a spammer distribution chain and your computer might start sending spam messages.
10. The sender information should always be checked of suspicious messages. Spammers usually use falsified email addresses for sending emails to conceal the actual sender. They will send the emails in the BCC field for hiding the huge number of recipients.

11. You should be extra careful while setting up auto replies as they may verify your email address as a valid email address to the spammers.
12. You should always weed out the addresses that you feel are inappropriate when forwarding a mail to a group of people. It is wise to add all of the recipients in the BCC field. This will hide them from one another.
13. You can make use of firewall software on your system for stopping attacks from spammers who attempt to compromise your computer and use it for sending more spam messages.
14. When you receive a spam message, always remember to examine the message headers. They probably are spam messages if they look like a jumble of random domains and servers.
15. Select stronger user names or alliances, as easy or short aliases are more prone to spam messages compared to longer and unusual aliases. For making a strong or an unusual alias you can make use of special characters like hyphens, underscores and periods. But you should see that the service provider allows the special characters.
16. You should not use your real email addresses for downloading free stuff or for signing up online.
17. Never make purchases that are based on the received spam messages. This will cut the economic foundation of spammers.
18. You should avoid using the same email address for multiple services. In the place of your email address, you can use disposable addresses on email Aliases.
19. You should not use the message preview option, if external images on scripts are displayed on it. These

elements might send your information in background to the sender.
20. You should avoid using the same username on different domains. Using the same username will make it easier for the spammers to find you on other services.

In most of the cases, for sending spam mails, the spammers will need to know your email address. By keeping your email address to yourself and by limiting your email address to your work purposes, you can reduce the amount of spam you get.

Chapter 9 - Downloads And Online Fun

Although you probably hear the word "download" every day and think of this as a normal activity on websites, be very careful. What a download means is that you are allowing a program to run on your computer. Although it may be a program that you really want to try, be careful during the installation period. The manufacturer may not have asked you for money, but if it's a free program, chances are that there are catches. When the installation program asks if you want all of the add-ons, be sure to tick boxes to say that you don't want them, or un-tick boxes as appropriate.

The problem is that many of these are Trojan Horses and bring things onto your computer that you don't particularly want, need or desire. If you have taken my previous advice about installing K9, you will be told to look out when you try to install anything that could be potentially harmful. Even on games websites, read the small print before you download anything.

If you want to be safe when you are on the Internet, set all your browsers to private settings so that others will not gain access to your information. There's a great piece of information on doing this for all browsers, which can be found [here](http://www.computerhope.com/issues/ch001378.htm).

Protecting your data

In a dishonest age, use memory sticks or portable hard drives to keep all of your data stored, so that it's not on your computer. Then if a laptop gets stolen, the thief does not have access to this information. This is very important indeed but it also means that key loggers and people who are watching your activity are unable to use the data because it's not actually stored on the computer.

The data gained by key loggers is vital to your security. For example, if you use a keyboard, they can actually trace the words typed. Although it's not completely foolproof, you can use what's called a virtual keyboard , which is great on a tactile screen such as that provided by the iPad, as these taps are unlikely to be broken into information that can be used against you.

Chapter 10: Keyloggers

Whether it is called monitoring software, spyware or a keylogger, these are equivalent of the digital surveillance, which reveals every touch and click, every conversation and download. A keystroke logger or a keylogger in short, is of software, which tracks and logs in the keys that are pressed on your keyboard. All this will be done in a covert manner without the user knowing that his actions are being monitored. Keyloggers are usually used for collecting account information, usernames and passwords, credit card numbers and any other private or sensitive data.

Although all of these uses are illegitimate, there are also legitimate uses of keyloggers. Keyloggers can be used by parents to monitor the online activities of their children, it can be used by law-enforcement for analyzing and tracking the incidents that are linked to the usage of personal computers, and the employers can check on their employees if they are working instead of browsing the Internet all day.

Nevertheless, the usage of keyloggers always poses a serious threat to the users as password can be easily intercepted and any confidential information, which is entered using the keyboard, can be obtained. Cyber criminals can use these keyloggers for obtaining account numbers and PIN codes of the user's financial accounts, passwords to your social networking accounts and emails. They can use the obtained information for stealing your identity, for financial transactions from your accounts and can even extort money and information from your family and friends.

How would one get a keylogger?

Keyloggers are just like any other malicious programs; keyloggers are also spread pretty much in the same way. You can exclude cases where a jealous partner or spouse installs these keyloggers. Just visiting a site that is infected, a keylogger can be installed on your computer.

On the contrary of what you know, the usages of keyloggers are not just limited to spying on your online activities. A keylogger can capture your keystroke in any program which is offline or online. So if you think you can type your password safely in WordPad or a notepad, and then copy and paste it on the web form, would really not work.

How can one detect a keylogger?

It is not easy to detect a keylogger. But there are some signs with which you can detect a keylogger on your computer or any other device. The performance will be slower when browsing the web, sometimes your keystrokes and mouse pause for a moment or sometimes they don't show up on the screen in the way you are actually typing. Receiving messages when loading web pages or graphics can also mean the existence of a keylogger.

There are three main types of keyloggers identified by the NIST scientists:

Hardware

The hardware keyloggers are small in-line devices that are placed in between the computer and the keyboard. As they are small, they usually go undetected, sometimes even for very long periods of time. These tiny devices are capable of capturing thousands of keystrokes, which may include email and banking usernames and passwords. For cyber criminals, the threat of getting caught for breaching the device is a deterrent. Keylogger can be placed in the hardware device that connects the keyboard on your desktop. There are a few hardware keyloggers that are placed inside the keyboard itself. Software cannot detect the hardware keyloggers. The drawback of hardware keyloggers is that they should have a physical access to the device. If you think there is a hardware keylogger installed on your computer, the best solution is to inspect your keyboard or you can even replace it.

Software

By using the SetWindowsHookEx function, which monitors every keystroke, Keylogging can be performed. There will be two different files in the package in which one of them is an executable file, which will initiate the hook function, and the second is a DLL file, which handles the logging functions. Even the auto complete password can be traced by the application that calls the function SetWindowsHookEx. Form filling software like RoboForm, which store information like credit card info, passwords and other information in the database. This software will later enter this information to the web forms as needed. With this, the user need not type all the data every time he tries to login and the need of using the keyboard is eliminated. Using software like this will prevent the hacker from getting the information. This is not completely safe either. There spywares that are capable of intercepting the data posted by the form fillers into the forms.

Kernel/driver

This kind of keylogger goes all the way down to the kernel level and it can intercept the data from an input device, like the keyboard directly. For intercepting the keystrokes, this kind of keylogger will replace the core software. This keylogger can be programmed in such a way that it cannot be detected virtually. Executing this software when the device is turned on and before the execution of any uses your level application can do it. As they run on the kernel level, even the operating system cannot detect it and it stays virtually invisible to it. For monitoring and recording the keystrokes, other keyloggers use hooks into the keyboard API of the operating system. Keyloggers usually send their log files covertly back to their masters either by using FTP or via email. There is an advantage for this approach. As this runs on the kernel level, it cannot log the password if it is filled by the autocomplete, as this will be performed in the application layer. Though there are a few advantages of keyloggers where parents can use them for monitoring the browser history of their children or employers monitoring their employees' productivity levels, there are also malicious keyloggers like the Zeus Trojan, which steals everything from highly suggestive research, corporate data and banking credentials. These kind of malicious keyloggers are showing up everywhere.

Defending Against Keyloggers

There are many kinds of defenses with which you can prevent the Keyloggers from stealing your information.

Physical Security: You must always consider physical protection of the computer. Whether the computer is at home, in an office or during traveling, keeping the computer secure and making sure no one has access to it is a primary concern.

Application Whitelisting: In this method, all the software that are approved will be placed in the *whitelist* and any other software will be prevented from being downloaded onto your device. For fighting against malware and viruses, this is an effective and emerging approach. A list of safe software called the *whitelist* will be given to the computer and any other software will be instructed to be blocked.

Many computer experts think that this approach is far more superior when compared to the standard signature based, antivirus approach of removing/blocking software that is harmful. The standard approach generally means that the exploits are already on the spread.

Detection Software: it is an anti-keylogger programed which will attempt to detect and disable the keylogger programs on a computer. An anti keylogger program will scan the hard disk and searches for the digital signatures of already existing keyloggers. It will also scan for the low-level software hooks. These hooks indicate if there is a keystroke grabber present. When compared to the normal antivirus software, the keylogger detectors and anti keyloggers are a lot better at detecting the keyloggers as the antivirus identifies the keyloggers as malware. You should not forget that the keyloggers could also be used for legitimate purposes.

Here are some tips for home users, which will help you to prevent the infection.

For home users, the additional tips to help prevent infection are:

- You should always be careful when you are going on the Internet. The drive-by downloads from the ads which are linked with malware are found on popular news sites.
- At a minimum, at least have anti-virus and antispyware loaded, and make sure they're kept up to date. Again, buy from a reputable vendor;
- You can switch to a virtual machine when you are online and can browse the Internet.

Virtual machines are divided into two major categories based on their degree of correspondence and the use to any real machine. A complete system platform which supports the functioning and execution of an actual operating system provided by the system virtual machine. The second type of virtual machine is the process virtual machine. Process virtual machines are designed in such a way that they run a single program. The software that runs inside is limited by the extractions that are provided by the virtual machine and the resources. They only stay inside of the virtual world and cannot break out of it. This is an essential characteristic of a virtual machine. You can keep the actual computer clean by clearing of the virtual machine on regular basis. Malware and viruses cannot be installed on the hard disk of the computer.

Anti-Keylogging Software Options

KeyScrambler is an anti keylogger design for the Windows operating system and it works a tad differently. As its name suggests, KeyScrambler are used for scrambling your keystrokes. They perform a driver level encryption and the software application will decrypt them. The result of using keystrokes is that they only see the keystrokes that are scrambled. Zemana AntiLogger Free is a free anti keylogger, which not only protects your web browser but every application that is present on your computer. This also uses a keystroke-encryption like the KeyScrambler for scrambling the keystrokes, protecting everything that is typed. Zemana is compatible with the Windows XP, Windows Vista, and Windows 7 or Windows 8 operating systems.

KL-Detector is free software, which detects keyloggers. It only detects them but does not remove them. The official page of KL-Detector says that it is only compatible with

Windows 2000 and Windows XP. If there is an anti-virus program on your computer, it may flag them as malware but you can ignore them.

There are a few anti-spyware programs, which are capable of detecting the keyloggers by their behavior or by their signature. For instance, any program that is on the keyboard API shown as a potential keylogger. Malwarebytes Antimalware, Spybot-Search & Destroy, Windows Defender, Ad-Aware and SUPER AntiSpyWare are a few general purpose anti malware applications, which have a keylogger detection abilities. When dealing with keyloggers, the final defense is a firewall. Firewalls can detect outbound traffic. Whenever there is an unauthorized attempt made to transmit data, the firewall will alert the user, which could possibly indicate that the keylogger is trying to contact the spammer it's a log file.

Chapter 11: Do's and Don'ts of Internet Security

1. Avoid using the same password for different accounts

In the present scenario, any given active participant of the Internet has anywhere up to a 10 to 20 online accounts. The online accounts could be in the form of email, social networking sites, online shopping sites, banking sites, meme sites, and video streaming sites or torrents download sites.

Since the number of accounts is too many, majority of the users won't even attempt to create a unique password for every account they have. They use the same password for all of their accounts, which is very convenient given the forgetfulness of an average Internet user. Also, you might have a favorite word or a phrase, which you have use as a password for many years. But, you should get out of the habit of using the same password for different accounts. Here's why- if a hacker gets hold of the password of one of your accounts, he can easily hack into the remaining accounts, since they all share the same password.

Yes, it is not easy setting a unique password for every account and then remembering it, but as they say, where there is a will, there is a way. Try coming up with a sentence or a phrase related to a particular account, which you can remember easily and cannot be possibly guessed by others; pick the first letter of every word in the sentence and add some digits at the end. Voila! You have a strong, bizarre looking password that doesn't make any sense, which is good because no one can possibly guess it.

For example, let us say you have an account for online banking at the Bank of America website. Think of a phrase related to the site, which can be easily memorized, like-"The Bank of America lent me tuition fee in the year 2005". Now, pick the first letters of every word in the sentence and turn it into "tboalmtfity2005", which is a pretty strong password, as it cannot be found in a dictionary and cannot be possibly guessed. If it is an online shopping site like Amazon, think of something you relate to the site like- "I bought my blow dryer at Amazon for 20 dollars" and turn it into "Ibmbdaaf20d" which makes a pretty decent password too. So, pull your socks up, go nuts with your creativity and change your passwords.

2. Do not use simple passwords that are easy to guess

People tend to use simple passwords that are easy to remember like the names of dear ones and pets, birthdays or their favorite bands' names. The problem with choosing such passwords is that, they can be guessed easily or can be cracked within seconds using password-cracking tools. If you can find the words of your password in a dictionary, it means it can be cracked easily. Even worse, some people use passwords like "12345" "4567" "letmein", "password", "superman", "qwerty" etc; That is not a good practice at all. Showing some creativity while setting passwords for your accounts wouldn't hurt. Here is a ridiculous list of the top 25 of the most commonly used passwords:

1. password	10. dragon	19. shadow
2. 123456	11. baseball	20. 123123
3. 12345678	12. 111111	21. 654321
4. qwerty	13. iloveyou	22. superman
5. abc123	14. master	23. qazwsx
6. monkey	15. sunshine	24. michael
7. 1234567	16. ashley	25. football
8. letmein	17. bailey	
9. trustno1	18. passw0rd	

Passwords and Password Managers

If you feel that you can't manage and remember the passwords for all of your accounts, a password manager comes to your aid. It is nothing but software that aids a user in storing and organizing passwords. The user needs to create a very strong master password, for gaining access into the password database. Password managers may either store the passwords in the cloud or on the user's pc itself. Even though the main duty of a password manager is to store and maintain the password with high security, most of them provide additional functionalities like generating passwords and form filling.

The advantage of using a password manager is that, every time you try to log into an account, it creates a random password that is alpha numeric and 20 characters in length.

Such a strong password drastically reduces the chances of your account being hacked.

Some password managers can also be used for the automatic filling of login field after comparing the URL of the site you are currently visiting with the stored URL of the site. If the URLs do not match, then the automatic filling of the login form does not take place. This feature protects the users from fake websites that imitate the real websites in design. With this added advantage, it is beneficial and advised to use the password manager software, even if you maintain only a few passwords. Thus, these password managers can safeguard the user from entering into a phishing site.

3. Be wary of strangers online

You don't have to be so generous while accepting friend requests or invitations on social media sites. Do not accept requests from strangers. Do not trust people you do not know so easily. If you suspect someone is stalking you, block them.

4. Lost your phone? Erase the data remotely

Many smart phones provide features like 'Android Lost', 'Find My iPhone', or 'BlackBerry Protect" which let the users remotely wipe away all the personal data on their phones, in case they are stolen or lost. Even if you hadn't signed up for the feature prior to the loss or theft of your phone, most of the times, you can still implement the feature after you lost your phone.

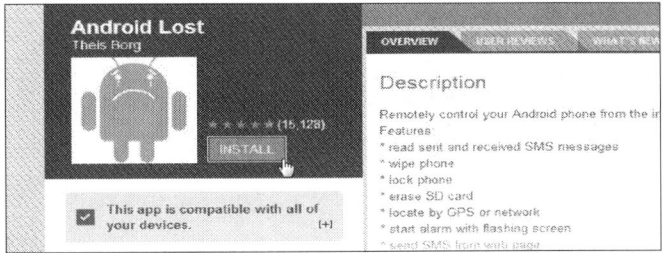

5. Look for the closed lock icon during online transactions

Look for a closed lock icon on your web browser while performing online transactions. This icon (or an unbroken key icon) indicates that the transaction is happening in a secure mode. The lock icon opens if you are not on a secure communication anymore.

6. Never respond to pop-ups

You must be familiar with pop-ups that say you are the 10,000,000th visitor of a site or that you have won a free iPhone and that all you need to do is click on a link to claim your prize. Never ever respond to such pop-ups. Most often, these pop-ups lead to malicious websites, which trick users into giving away information like their contact details, email id or even worse, credit card details. Some pop-ups will download malware in the background, infecting your computer and data. Also, ignore pop-ups that invite you to take part in 'annual visitor survey' or other surveys, unless you want to install malware onto your system. The best thing to do is enable pop-up blockers in your web browser.

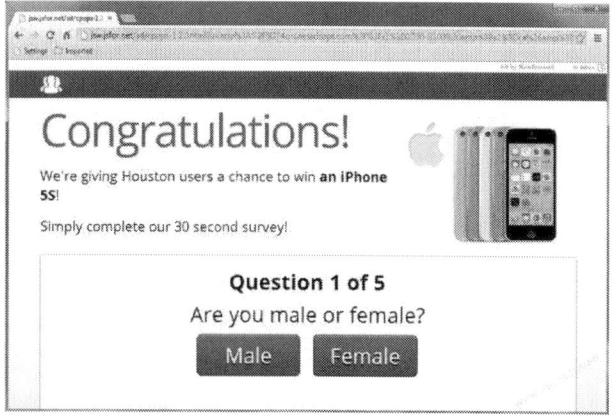

7. Maintain more than one email account

Don't use a single email account for everything. Create an email account for every purpose, for example, set aside an email account for personal mails, another one for online shopping or ticket booking, one for online banking, one for work related mails etc; That way, even if one account gets hacked, the rest of the accounts remain untouched. Also, phishing mails can be easily spotted this way. For example, let us suppose you receive an email from your bank to your email account meant for online shopping. You can easily make out that it is a fake, as you have not submitted this email address to your bank.

8. Go for two-step verification

Do set up a two-step verification, if your email service or social networking account offers it. In the two-step verification, the first step involves entering a correct password. In the second step, a verification code is messaged to your mobile, which you need to enter for logging in. That way, even if a hacker cracks your password, he will not be able to enter the verification code required for logging in. Gmail users need to undergo the two-step verification only once in every 30 days or when they attempt to sign in from a different device.

9. Keep your phones and tablets locked

See that a password or PIN number locks your phones and tablets. It could be a bit of a hassle for you to enter a password every time you want to use your phone, but it is your first line of defense against hackers.

Conclusion

Thank you for downloading our book and we hope that it has helped you in some way to keep your family safe while using the Internet. It's not expected that you will take all this information in at the first read. However, if you go back through the pages, you will find that you will gain little snippets about keeping yourself safe and will gain more confidence when you start to use them.

It's extremely important that you do keep yourself safe. Your passwords, for example, should be updated regularly and should consist of small letters, large letters and numbers in a combination that isn't easy to remember. Don't use the same passwords for all of the websites that you access as this makes it very easy for thieves to get into every account that you log into just by knowing that one password.

It's a pretty scary place out there and if you take all the actions shown in this eBook you can keep yourself safe from harm. Make sure your home computer connectivity is set to a private network. When using a router, this will be the manufacturer's setting, so you don't need to worry about it too much. That means you have to give a pass code to people who want to use that network. If anyone can gain access to your network or connect to the Internet through your router without asking you for this information, then your router settings may not be as secure as you imagine them to be. Check with your Internet service supplier and ensure that they are secured.

The Internet isn't all bad news. There are so many opportunities out there for people to enjoy. This book is written for those readers who really want to make their Internet experience as hassle free and safe as possible. If you follow the guidelines, you really cannot go that far wrong and you can continue to keep safe while working on your computer. Do update your virus protection. Do make sure that you don't speak to strangers or give information that gives you any risk of security in email. Be safe, be aware and enjoy what the Internet was intended for.

RECOMMENDED READING

Hacking: Hacking For Beginners and Basic Security: How To Hack

hyperurl.co/hacking

MIND CONTROL:

Manipulation, Deception and Persuasion Exposed

Hyperurl.co/mindcontrol

Android: App Development & Programming Guide: Learn In A Day!

hyperurl.co/androids

PSYCHOPATH: Manipulation, Con Men And Relationship Fraud

smarturl.it/psychoa

JAVA: Java Programming, JavaScript, Coding: Programming Guide: LEARN IN A DAY!

hyperurl.co/javaos

Printed in Great Britain
by Amazon